HEARSAY

HEARSAY

CHRISTOPHER ANKNEY

Washington Writers' Publishing House
Washington, D.C.

COVER DESIGN AND PHOTO by Ashley Hornish
AUTHOR PHOTO by Lynn Ankney
TYPESETTING by Barbara Shaw

LIBRARY OF CONGRESS CATALOGUING-IN-PUBLICATION DATA
Ankney, Christopher
    [Poems. Selections]
    Hearsay / Christopher Ankney.
       pages cm.
    ISBN 978-1-941551-01-1 (pbk : alk. paper)
    I. Title.
    PS3601.N55454A6 2014
    811'.6—dc23
                                        2014010388

Printed in the United States of America

WASHINGTON WRITERS' PUBLISHING HOUSE
P. O. Box 15271
Washington, D.C. 20003

ACKNOWLEDGMENTS

I am very thankful to the following journals and their editors for giving fine homes to the poems, in some cases at different stages of their lives:

Boxcar Poetry Review — "Catching Beauty" originally appeared as "Waltz Down Rue Des Halles"

Burnside Review — "The Last Living Primitives"
"[The boy's French was beautiful as skipping stones]" originally appeared as "[The boy's French was beautiful as skipping rocks]"

Conte — "Catfish On The Maumee"

Copper Nickel — "Lake Victoria"

Crab Orchard Review — "Churches"

Fourteen Hills — "Namesake"

Gulf Coast — "To Recession:"

Harpur Palate — "Miscarriages"
"To The Housepainter:"

Hayden's Ferry Review — "Physiology"
"The Moons Clings To The Morning"

Hunger Mountain — "The Boundaries Of Science"

The Journal — "The Golden One"

Linebreak — "To Failure:"

The Los Angeles Review — "When I Was A Boy The Sun Was A Horse"

The Louisville Review — "Sun Peels The Skin Off A Barn"

Lunch Ticket — "1988: Suicide"

MARGIE — "Necropolis"

Nashville Review — "Venus De Milo"

New Madrid — "Foreclosure"
"The Best Peaches Came From An Old Black Woman Who Hated My Mother"

Prairie Schooner — "Father Belongs To The River"

Slipstream — "At The Museum Of Natural History"

Sou'wester — "Patches"

storySouth — "To Mockery:"

Temenos — "American Travel"

Third Coast — "To The Rivers:"

Tupelo Quarterly	"Could Have Been"
	"[I Solemnly] Swear"
Zone 3	"Brother Tongue"

Thank you to everyone at Washington Writers' Publishing House for selecting my collection for the Jean Feldman Poetry Prize. A special thanks to Robert Herschbach, Holly Karapetkova, Brandel France de Bravo, Sid Gold, and Kathleen Hellen for their editorial insights. Thank you to Patric Pepper and the rest of the press in guiding the book into production, as well.

Thank you to James Reiss, my mentor, whose works and stern approbation have kept my eyes starboard for more than fourteen years. Thank you to David Schloss and the rest of the Miami University English Department. Thank you to David Trinidad for all of his influence. Thank you to Crystal Williams and Joan Larkin for the depth and kindness of their MFA workshops at Columbia College Chicago. Thank you to Tony Trigilio and Peter Christensen. To Western Michigan University's Prague Summer Program, thank you for blessing me with the chance to work with Mark Jarman, whose advice in and out of workshop is evident throughout this book, and with Alicia Ostriker, sage and precise. Thank you to Ishai Barnoy, Lauren Arnsman, Jason Olsen, and Naoise Hefferon. Thank you to Cora Jacobs. Thank you to Michael Collier and Eduardo Corral. Thank you to the Defiance Public Library and its collections of Robert Frost. To my family and dearest friends: my love and thanks.

Principally, thank you to Brian Russell, a true *Wunderkind*, as others have rightly called him. These poems would be too scared to get up and sing if it were not for you.

Most importantly, thank you, Lynn. I am the man, the husband, the father I am because I have you. Thank you for Robin, and thank you to Robin.

CONTENTS

iii.

for Robin J. Letso

|

22 Oct. 1956 – 21 Oct. 1988

i.

…that he weighed more than any dead man they had ever known,
almost as much as a horse, and they said to each other that maybe
he'd been floating too long and the water had got into his bones.

– Gabriel Garcia Marquez,
  "The Handsomest Drowned
  Man in the World"

WHEN I WAS A BOY THE SUN WAS A HORSE
for James Reiss

Clouds were a dreamer's sheep, pure
white or devilishly gray.

Ponds were always the La Brea tar pits
trying to swallow more beasts.

Every forest my father's hidden kingdom.
Every half-buried tire, piece of litter, rusted bike frame

a magical clue in the three-year crusade
between his vanishing act and salvage –

found cracked to pieces at the foot of a wall
a kingdom an hour down river.

What was left of the body a litany
of punctuation.

On the drought-riddled beach
at Clear Lake the next summer, hundreds

of choked walleyes littered the sand –
and we two boys imagined them as plagued

soldiers of Normandy. Stuck in crawls,
their lips blue petals in bloom

for the soul's escape – pulled to shore
by boat-waves and a hot round

of adrenaline meant to grease
the body's machinery

into action – so many boys awakened
in June's hot stampede.

THE BOUNDARIES OF SCIENCE

We are earthbound lovers suffocating from the gravity
        of earthbound situations: so I confess to terrible thoughts: snapping

rude necks, stabbing myself in the eye with a fork; testing the boundaries
    of the electric fence
        that is our bodies: our nervous
systems.

I confess to watching strangers through glass
and holding stares until everyone looks down at their feet.

I confess to the cow's eye senior year, empty sight,
the cornea peeled: the delicate stream
of vitreous humor into metal tray puddle: nothing away from its body

but salt water: a harbor: a gulf of vision: a hurricane tossing rods
and cones: capsizing
                    the monotony of the scientific method.

All of it: I confess: a thunderbolt of anger in punching the blind
driver's car and spitting on his plates: for his reminding me

how pliant is life: a love:

I confess that we are compatible contradictions: peg and peg hole: temper
and temper: lit flare and salty ocean: the rib and rib eater; the robin the owl.

We are a March night spent in a tent, frosted by a dying season: the doe the buck
        at the forest edge, waiting for the earth to bury the cold.

We are the rivers joined at the fort.
We are readers of the sky. *And even if we scatter*

to the stars,
isn't it likely that we may take our problems with us
or find, later, that they have followed us?

You who opens a book and reads like the hare: but damns the tortoise
        for each worded step: you who will open your mouth and snap
with the jaw of the tortoise:
but choke out a fire with sand when it snaps

at your skin: your beautiful, earthly skin. Your beautiful, earthly eyes: mouth: mind.

1988: MURDER

He hides under my bed and taps a knife
on night's pipes
    until my hand's sliced
            down to fatty roots,
       opening
a can
of peaches: deadened
where pain should exist.
         I try to reshape the wound.

Four stitches and two weeks
        showering with hand flapping
in air
    like an operatic puppet, striving
for anthemic notes
nobody ever conquers.

This faceless unsub, Oklahoma myth:
    not cowboy or schooner
            pioneer: an addict
treacherous enough to bullwhip
a friend into yoke.

   If I am you, Father, this conjurer does not hold me
gunpoint.
     Time does not blur truth to the magic
            audience:
nature does not saw
my body
into its cruelest pieces.

   I sign *HELP ME* on the withdrawal slip
before hope drains
   up the plastic tube
to the teller. I transact escape
         with subtlety, prepared

for the probable: surviving underwater
        with carp, bottom-feeders
that won't discern
bread-balls from flesh.

Your body: failed, clean
        down to its bones. My body answers the Y
to the ME:

        lets awe spill
                        from the scalpel's mouth
as it inspects
        sternum to pubic,
                    skin peeled back for directions
                                to the body's brutal ending.

        There is no burial
of knowledge, sleight
of hand, petrifying
waters.

I am Houdini: reveal myself
before the audience
        loses consciousness of the trick
                                being played
on them, too.

TOTEM: 1991

Your power animal emerged from the Maumee: blue-point
Siamese: imperial Angkor Wat warrior
                            wet and crooning on a crashed raft
                fashioned out of canal lock a century out of fashion.

This same year your jawbone was used
                to identify what was you: imperishable crowns

and your wallet: the swollen river
                                            receded, its withholding of who, defeated

by dental taxonomy: by the mountains built in your mouth.

Both of us abandoned
                during this first fishing expedition: just settled in
your old neighborhood, clueless to paradox. Your teeth slashing
                                            our collarbones, as if defending the temples

from British occupation: The Beatles mangled
by the walkman's loose wiring
                                    between ears: half-blood brother
rehearsing
            how to add to his ark of five cats, hen, and dog:

the root of never wanting

        to smell like I wasn't good enough to keep their eyes
                                            on the register
while I thumbed my way
            through books   or returned the unchosen
unaffordable clothes
            back to the sale rack.

It only took your howling prayer
on a fractured pillar
                to capture us: tyrant king

of my heart: of Kingsbury Park:
it would take the strength of Samson to crumble

those locks: so we crowned you such: just
or not. Your hiss a growl: cowered
                                    the dog, chained to flagpole
in the backyard, jealous of your alley-cat sovereignty.

When we banged
the backboard, Bulls crest ablaze, you guarded
from the garage roof, swatted
        our nearest shots.

We knew we couldn't keep you
        from running off

whenever you had the desire to slay a lion.

We were Philistines in this town,
        and you were the strength of God, killing
                who we were: wedlock boys: bastard rats.

You came back so many times
I thought you always would. Hero
through existence
in words: in a silly cat.

For decades, drowned in myths: we forge *father* like earth

into fire-makers: from crumpled Hellas
to flat Kansas, *thunder* comes from the mouth

        to warn us of impending doom. We are the biggest tools
of everywhere. We are everywhere

                            wanting to be creationists and wanting
                to be cradled by the invisible:
the disappeared make us doubt

what we are. I know men
who laugh at dolphins
mourning: who find computers life.

We can believe Elvis still lives:
we can believe Zeus' head split:
Harrison Ford's a cranky god:
I'll take a father anywhere
I can: from the rotating wheel
that followed your death to
the teachers who leveled the earth
with compassion. The Celts
made a god of taverns: Acassbel!
Ogun is a metalsmith in tribal
Togo. Lab coats and Anishnaabeg
believe we rose from saltwater.

Everywhere a circle exists as holy. Facts dilute like salt.

                You have died again

and again as I have retold for a quarter
                        century, your exodus.

I can still hear the purr: soft engine
            of what I want to believe
a love that trembles waters

all the way back to the fantastical, elaborate barays
                        of Siam, past what we firmly grasp:

the mind more capable than the hands
of carving out reverence: enveloping beliefs

        that we cannot father ourselves

in human form without precedence or presence
of a spirit guide: without becoming
the earth itself.

SUN PEELS THE SKIN OFF A BARN

A soft brooding of crop-dust accents
the lower sky, the backdrop a forest:
one freckle on the sun-drenched face of earth.
    I hear old voices say, *Drink this in*: a slow chug
of two-way, highway traffic; the open land's cry
for childhood to come back. All that big steel
churning, and nothing but a little dirt released
by the combine: its massiveness: its mass.
    As kids we licked up all we could of the fields,
played house and city in barns; watched
big rubber tires smash the land back into itself
as it swallowed corn and bean into the belly
of the tractor, leaving rows of chewed-on
golden stalks.
    But the sun's a lamp, and this seasonal prayer
evoked in the car, now, makes more
of the nothing:
    an old neighbor convinced the sky
a kind of god's lens, a spotlight
over farmers and their sagged, sleepy barns.
    And, in a way, we are right to hear
the wind's cold advice to love decay
as he tucks us in and flips the switch –
then leaves us all to shiver.

TO THE RIVERS:

You cut the city like a wishbone.
You carry a thousand small vigils in your pockets, your waves.

You are a point on a fort map in 1812.
An apple tree is drawn where Pontiac Park now ramps into your mouth.

My uncle, local legend, skis barefoot in festival season; shaves your rough skin.
Walt Whitman believes in your beautiful lie, in return.

Could you spit back the drunken half-boy, who tackled other half-boys for
     scholarship?
The cops chased him into your mouth; bitten by December's quiet teeth, they
     stepped back.

He was eighteen, which means nothing to your cutting.
What can you say to his mother's apple-tart lips?

They call you Maumee and Auglaize. Indian and white.
They call you a confluence, a junction, once Ohio's end.

My father, my mother says, had Indian in him.
His history walks into you, too.

I ride my bike along you, who broke the canals; left them. The locks we cast off.
My brother and I have taken little back: carp, crappie, catfish.

This is what we have left. Hands cupped, pre-school, a robin's shell pulled to earth.
I have his name, Robin, in my palms, and it is a soft blue.

You are a mini-shipbuilder, shaping new colors out of twigs.
You are a meeting place. A thousand natives canoed from Fallen Timbers, westward.

You know if their last breaths were in your arms, or on land where life can anchor
     the strongest.
You pulled them into your chest, where the cannons pointed east; where the library
     now breathes.

When I am back, I spend mornings with a book, reading you.
The sky lightens and your muddy skin shimmers.

You are not alive. You do not see your complicities.
You are a gun sending its prey down the plank.

LAKE VICTORIA

And we have
science to keep up its pedantic fight
to bare the intricacies of our daily motion –
why we flip one leg out of bed, then
the other; why we wash our hands
through a stream of morning rays
as we adapt our eyes from the fishbowl
blur of the bedroom, shaded and private.

Each day brings the same self-knowledge
and a thousand new things we didn't know
we need to know about ourselves.

Today it goes beyond water
though it includes. In Lake Victoria,
deep in the genes of mother Uganda,
father Tanzania, humans are sloshing
waist high in rubber clothes,
a bit primitive in their research.

They are deep in our past, holding buckets
of red male flesh. They find women fish
are cutting through an underworld
attracted to those bodies on a wavelength
of colored light.

Water prisms the surface, filters
their world into red or blue – those classics
used most in flags, in honor, in bravery.

They have a theory on making choices.
The hypothesis: the deeper the murkier.

BROTHER TONGUE

We said it was hella salty
when little Mario
called us crackers.

We said it was bloody salty
when the Diamondback bit
our shins with its metal pegs.

Your best friend Neil was full
of salty in every music video
not parading Marilyn Manson

in prosthetic breasts. He was
dope salty. The rest, salty
dopes. We wore flannel

on our lips. Cobain filled us
like shakers. Our youth risen
out of pain, shared meals

of salty. Neil's father timed
beatings. Salty, bro. Your
father, run off down South:

salty as all hell. People furrowed
at our salties – we drowned them
in more salty. All boys pour

a quiet language on wounds,
but it doesn't burn. Our world
salty: I double-dare you, look back.

TO MOCKERY:

Think of those dumb letters slipped in the gills
        of her locker freshman year.
                She was the toughest catch,
the dearest homecoming queen-to-be,
wasn't she.

Remember when twenty-six cats slept under the skirt
        of our trailer, behind the front steps
              where the hem was torn.
No one wants to be known as the kid with fleas
jumping off his MC Hammer-pants.

When my dad disappeared he died quickly in me.

And when his outline was pressed
              into the leafy floor, half eaten
by the world in those three years, of a naked October
forest, he awoke in my lungs
                  and has never left.

He was awkward. I think he sits in my bones
and makes me awkward, too.
              My mother says

I'm growing into his face; though I took her eyes

I can't give mine to my own children.
The eyes come from the mother.

I *am* okay. I willingly give up this body, like a sexual act.
Its delicate badges, the ease of bruises blooming into a jade spring;

I would rather dress myself in the river
  and its repulsive currents. I'd rather be a river
that carves its way again and again,

and never settles enough
to have a clear face picked
from the day's criminal lineup.

Wear the narrow stories of me on your tongue
        if you must – your little charades.
Leave me the roots. Leave me the peace of the forest

floor. I'll give you anything else –
anything more.

TO RECESSION:

We can hang our winter coats on the rack –
          the earth has wiped its eyes, yawned

and peeled the snow off
in its slow exhalations.
               From Ohio to Illinois,
deer gather in fields, eight to ten in every open, sallow patch.
          The small crowds press their noses
like the first people at the concert; early to the front.

Baby calves imitate small black rocks, curled
          tired in the grass
from wobbly legs spinning
               like four tops.

The priest says God will bring me to the Catholic Church;

          he doesn't have to do a thing.

We need to push ourselves
          to recycle more, and listen to the cold hard facts of ice.

The river has receded; the winter sheets have broken
          back into its bones. There's little to say but that

ice is redundantly inarticulate; its cracking speaks for us all.

The ice cubes in my sweet tea drown
because a hot breath blows on them from all sides.

Another floater was brought in from the river.
Drunk at 2am, he was taken in by the air's warm song.

His body was found near the school bus
               garage, by an anonymous man
in a small-engine fishing boat

who understands the current drags
      the powerless in a predictable path.

PATCHES

His lurch figure an effigy of the city on the bridge – Rewired,
you said, After the fire, you said – Mother – Don't touch

him, you said. But the car was always moving and so
were we. From a house by the dirty Maumee to another

house by the river's gut, where another river punched it –
where men were taken in, punch drunk, drunk or just punched –

What the city takes; stories on a raging tongue – the pervert
mayor, The Cat Lady and her red wagon – Patches, stitched

wool jacket – knees buckled from the bridge's sway, I thought, scared
of man's inventions of movement – I saw myself, the elevator

a box to heaven or hell – this tiny bridge a cement tightrope
for the sideshow, his arms planed for a soft landing –

and in the distance, summer, boats slipping into the river
at Pontiac dock. He's taking in the sky – He must be burning,

but you said, He can't feel a thing. You said he's homeless
and simple. You said he couldn't put it together

that he's in this world. You said, One more flood
and we're moving again. And yet, we stayed. Stay.

CATFISH ON THE MAUMEE

"And catfish twist through the bones
Of what never bothered to rise."
— *from* "I. The Ohio," Joe Bolton

Your body is wrapped in his barbels,
drug across the muddy floor
away from the asthmatic blue sky

inhaler, pulled by the colossal fish
through a cloud of exploding dirt —
poof — you are sunk by a last drink
of the river.

You are pulled far enough
each rescue spills through my hands
like water —

How long will I chase the bottom?
We can't know the view from there

until we are stupid or unlucky
or just too old and tired. Then an absence
of gills won't matter —

I laugh at the fish as my bare toes cut
the surface current,

because fish are stupid enough
they eventually wear down
out of hunger, curiosity, or pure
stumbling in the dark;

eventually, they nibble
at anything in their way, even toes.

This is some kind of revenge,
Sport, echoes the absent bank
as I jerk the line to paralyze
his fight.

I drag him up – awed lips –

to choke on the burdens of breathing –
his whiskers – taste buds
sensing death like defiant tongues,

stuck out as if to say, *We took your father*
for this. I cower on the rock, crawl up
to see an empty swing swinging,

kick-started by the wind, and each second
ticks off its pendulum:

I wake to the forest's requiem:
the coyote eating chickens
from the neighbor's coop; naturally,
howling.

FORECLOSURE

Yellow brick house of childhood,
chipped white paint off the backboard dangling
from garage –

How many windows shattered
by my wild lefty fastball?

Peering out the kitchen blinds
watching you, older brother, catwalking
backwards, from bedroom
down the gravel drive –
Cavalier, stealing the Cavalier! –

At fifteen! –

Oh, nimble feet – the adagio of growing
into different men in the same world –

you thought I was gay for knowing
what it means to *échappé*

but I sought the sensuality of French class
with quiet, awkward hope
that girls would swell over my tongue.

Oh, hope – we had it. American
as cinema –

Thank God we learned quickly
not to seek the Wizard of Oz –
with no damn father –

Thank God, Mother,
someone else will take the burden
off our hands –

though men were built of boys, there –

we'll only waste the days left
following our hearts down the past.

1988: SUICIDE

All-American heroes in flames, my right hand a god
controlling the world's freedom while my left hand presses
the knob of the aerosol bomb – Aqua Net in all its hot purple
splendor – slips, and Duke and Snake Eyes nearly collateral
damage to Voltar's char-bubbled plastic skin. No miracle
will get our mother to buy another Voltar. He's dead, she said.
Resurrection is imagination to innocence. We built the base
out of a tin can, walls raised from crayons, broken pencils:
a child's revival. Inside, the paratrooper closes my mother's
door, slowly, and gives us a once-over. He tells us how monkeys
threw shit at them when they landed in the jungle. We landed
in this shithole of a trailer after the drunk lost his house. Men
imagined themselves our father for three weeks at a time.
Not once did they resurrect my father, blown away
one October. We were tracing the topography of the states
of emotion. My sister says he walked himself into a hole
dug by prairie dogs – that they were evil fuckers and he tripped
on their drugs, sold everything in the house. Mother coasted
the back alleys of Oklahoma City, toward Ohio, when she flipped
the van as I swam in her belly. My sister says I should've been
retarded or dead. The white knight awoke from his methadone
slip up while Mother was on a morphine drip – doctors gave nine lives
to her pulp of leg. Like all fairy tales, the knight was trolled by trolls,
witches – the most damned spirits pulled him down the six years
he wanted to be Father. Too many times, he offered himself
to them like a buoy that doesn't know if it's the sea's savior
or just a fated object struggling to survive impossible waters.
The day before his thirty-third birthday, he vanished
like Jesus. Left us with myth. Left us dustless facts.
Clarity like a rain drop in the river. We translated days
into years. Years into men. In '92, a tornado brushed
the field, painted the harvest into a wheaten-skied Oz.
We followed the road; only, home was not a place
understood. Perhaps that's why my sister hates Dorothy.
If this version's truth, my father is the heartless Lion. If he baptized

himself in the river, how can I forgive? I was cradled
by these men because Mother wanted to apologize to somebody
for her guilt. And they wanted in her bedroom, so she told them
the secret to heroism was her children. They slipped
each time – like action figures unaware who really held the strings.

DAD:

I fell so far down the hole dug by Spades.
It's a tragedy I absolutely love

sweet tea, my tongue a sieve that craves
more and more sugar.

When I climbed the Guggenheim's spiral
I was conquering Dante's

Peak, Pierce Brosnan-style (one level
of badassness at a time).

I was twenty-one, a loaded water gun
lost in Kandinsky's playground, taiga white-top

geometrically too chichi for a Midwestern
boy. Your exodus beat hell into me,

stuck me on a hamster wheel, towing
sanity's horizon. Like cephalitis, your early exit

a virus sinking my little glass river shack.
I bobbed up and down like flotsam

into adulthood. The pros call it
bipolarity. You're going going gone

a rocket the bleacher crowd throws back.
The balls juiced, we'll never know the truth.

I always hear Elton John crooning,
Hold me closer, Tony Danza,

because he's *The Boss* and always sucked
the pain up under the rug and swung

at the pitcher's heat like the slugger he was,
while a *tiny dancer* just wears glittery skin

over tiny Bambi legs with giant Bambi eyes
staggered at the forest's blaze.

ii.

The end of man is knowledge, but there is one thing
he can't know. He can't know whether knowledge
will save him or kill him.

– Robert Penn Warren,
All The King's Men

AMERICAN TRAVEL

We're having trouble navigating maps
reviewed religiously in Social Studies
as we drive the neatly drawn paths
through these forests, London purchased
before survey and force. Cherokee roots
tracked to here, deeply buried in hearsay.
Something sometime somewhere
within these borders of American history
was said between a man and a woman
who likely had to ignore their elders to lie
with each other, forging a new line – its jagged
peaks and valleys like a cardiograph, bordering
in mountain cartography – our machines
put life into the appearance of order what we
lose easily so over short breaths of time.
Geologists must believe when we converge
destructive forces are at play: groundswell,
melted earth. Here, now, two plates long broken
into the Appalachians continue their clash
towards the sky. When we near the imaginary
state line, my son offers his coloring book,
asks me to choose the skin. The white pulp
admits to its manufacture on the page
while the DJ does her part, mocks Limbaugh:
thunderous shots echo off granite walls, exhaust
of two souped-up F350s dragging down
the Virginia highway – Why can't they fail to boast
Confederate flags? We're the ones scribing the world
with crayons. Outside, leaves are bronzed
by dusk; rocks glimmer like fool's
gold. The trees go on without us, vanish
into themselves given the chance
to be wild again.

MISCARRIAGES

Of justice, of course they've likely sought out why
God dropped stone relics in their bodies. To deliver
these thoughts to the world, though, a sign of weakness.

Or simply a third or fourth stab inside the belly.
Or simply too large a problem for anyone else
to tackle, or listen to. Confessions are to be whispered

in the solitary confinement of assembly lines,
where one only has time to think of going on
with the company order: noodles, tomatoes, bread

driven off to Indianapolis, Chicago, Cleveland.
So one grew into the "kooky" aunt who fed her remaining sons
as if fattening cattle, and they grew into college

football players. The second aunt: a tiny, powerful switch
of few words, a torture genius at barely five feet
who can contort an ear into the opposite of origami:

The hurt flies in place of the beautiful swan.
The third one leaves and returns as often as tornadoes
around Ohio: always, a minute's wreckage sets off

years of repair. Once, she brought a black man home
from Nebraska, and it was love and bruises
just as my uncles predicted. Only, their wives were tender

and housebroken, too. Only, my mom, rabid
of her surviving pups, snarled and showed
her teeth when she heard her brothers, having closed up

her heart for her boss – a black man a decade older,
with a Rolodex of lady names on his desk. Dignity fought for
at every holiday dinner. Then, there is sister night –

soaking in bathwater, not blessed enough to cleanse
what's lost. The ghosts crashing off skin, harsh music
that never escapes the sanctuary of the tub.

NAMESAKE

Like the Virgin Mary, you hang
saintly over the chair, captured in still life.

Sixteen, Renaissance blue sweater, a veil
ripening skin: skin to be ravished
by metal and glass shards, concrete and a century

old oak – the unmoving earth – when the car
flips like a penny. What young person can fathom
the cold physics of machinery: to know

a subtle shift of the wheel startles butterflies,
flutters them in droves from the cavernous horn?

Suddenly, everything can be renounced
by ravenous night: desperate sirens pulled your body
ashore from the mud-lake ditch. Dear Aunt I Never Knew:

the liturgy spreads from six sisters' mouths: a constellation
who find hardened solace in your heavenly escape: plague of bees
stinging in the form of childhood beatings and icy touches.

Tip-toes out the back door guided each girl
to some other troubled man who would teach her

more about the danger of cars, the immense horizon
that looks like flight from smallness, where she imagined
the clouds as chivalrous knights pulling the full moon down

to spotlight grazed fields, haunting country roads
where crickets and mistakes take center stage.
Where the lights engulfing the car in flames

are really a cop's sharp warning: on lookout
against the chill of uncovered, guiltless flesh.

THE BEST PEACHES CAME FROM AN
OLD BLACK WOMAN WHO HATED MY MOTHER

At first I shyly refused the peaches, their bitter
warmth one tastes at room temperature, flesh
loose but ready in the Indian summer.
She did not frown. Instead, she waved

to the kitchen and pointed at the sugar jar.
Her son told my mother's secret,
my sweet tooth would make me eat lima beans
if buried in confection. Those peaches turned

like Kryptonite, green to gold – less powerful –
and I lost the fight to hate her back
the way I heard her do my mother,
who could never marry her son

being a white whore. I hadn't owned my color
until I heard those words; never thought our poor
skin was that dirty, though I never felt clean living
in the trailer.

She used the heaping tablespoon topping
to fatten me with an unspoken forgiveness,
the way adults allow themselves to be bigger
when they dote on children.

Yes – the taste made me forget the foreignness
felt before like a slick intruder to the tongue.

WHEN TIN LUNCHBOXES WERE STYLISH

I think his name was Scott
        (or maybe that was the guy with the dog and the pool
                she left years after).
I missed the bus because she made breakfast
        and it's been twenty years now. Forgive me.
It was French toast, the burnt spots drowned faces
   in a purge of maple syrup.

Perhaps the glug of the bottle made her confess.

The clouds were always rising from cornfields on fall mornings,
from their dirt bed, as if tired of carrying the burden
of creation.

The leftover crop-stems scattered fields like hair
scissor-splayed from the scalps of my sister's Barbies.

Scott – we'll call him Scott – lifted her brush to his nose and sniffed.
He said he loved her strawberry hair, down to the small of her back.
She thinks he cleaned the brush into his pocket
        when she turned around.
                        She was sixteen; seventeen.

I'm in the third grade in the car. I'm watching black birds tight-rope
telephone wires.

I was wondering when or if the wires ended.
I was wondering if the giant wooden stakes stabbed the earth's heart

        or were deep enough to lead to China. (I'd seen that in a movie.
Jeff Goldblum and Cyndi Lauper – it was the '80s – took a hole
from America to China.)
               I think she was like Alice.

She saw a rotting tree next to an irrigation ditch.

     She said Scott loved her, but she said no. Her mother, later, swung a broom at him like a ninja. Swoosh.

He hung himself. It was done

     in a neighboring field; his body propped like a scarecrow.

She said a raven circled in the muck, and cawed and cawed.

WHAT WE LEARNED OF GOD

Off-stage trumpeting
commandments – bodiless voice
from cushy mount in the TV room –

Mother, hushed sidekick:
a plate must be cleared before an ass
can leave the kitchen

the yard demanded stripping
of every twig before we little birds
could flitter off to nest in the thin woods

bedrooms to be dusted of ghosts
of his grown children
before we could plot our own

stay out of his bedroom,
even if open, even if light

called our teething bodies to shore
or the silky blue expanse of the King –

gun found in his underwear drawer,
Magnum .57 – replaced,
we drowned

in detective stories on the bed's downy waves –
tried to hide our being there

broke into hives whispering
of the cold shaft, marble handle – trigger

frail as a sapling near bloom –
the violation of knowing
how easy it would be to crumple

a body like paper –
the thought charging from its dark cave
like an unbridled racehorse –

this world's wonders: portrait
of a black Jesus and Mary's
mahogany hands at center table –

a full set of NFL bobble-heads at attention
on four shelves: tiny painted smiles
underneath tiny painted masks,

glossy and immaculate –

our playing catch at this altar
sending tremors through the wall –

thirty angelic trolls – their infinite
nods – confessions
sung on springy necks

[THE BOY'S FRENCH WAS BEAUTIFUL
AS SKIPPING STONES]

The boy's French was beautiful as skipping stones
along a lake's shimmering surface. Just like a rock,
the words will eventually plop and sink,
the lake will gulp what touches its lips.

The lake is just a metaphor, like the whale
who swallowed Jonah. We are as small as plankton,
but the world keeps spitting us out.

The French boy is just a metaphor, like the world
we use in poems, just a word to grab our brothers
and sisters, pull them to our chests
with what feeble hands we have.

Hands have been a metaphor before.
The man in Sherwood Anderson's novel
about Ohio, where Ohio is just a metaphor
for America. And America is a simple man
who stands for the world. I remember how ugly

the man seemed, which is a metaphor
for the memories which sneak into
poems like teens at R-rated movies.

There were days I watched my mother snap
strangers' towels and jeans to a crisp fold, empty
the lint hatches from every dryer, mop the floors
and kiss the owner when the last lights were off.

Once our car pulled-up lame
next to the dumpster and I opened my door
to the limp body of a cat, its jaw agape,
its small teeth much sharper than any meaning
I can come to at the end of a day, my hands
blanketing the image of death.

I want to say the cat was really a rocket
red, plastic pencil box – the kind I used
in elementary school – and when the lid popped

at the laundry mat cash blew like a geyser:
I pulled a dollar from the crater,
bought myself a chocolate Moon Pie.

COULD HAVE BEEN

I *am* proud my gums have not melted like wax,
teeth barnacled like cave droppings, meth yellow.

It *is* impressive I have no intricate sleeves
inking the narrative: not even a cheeky tear drop

or gravestone sweating down the elbow
as I await another stranger to commence

the juicy bits tucked inside the numbers
and letters. My head is an answering machine.

Call it an absolute miracle I did not kill the cats
or hamsters as a boy.

I *didn't* hoard unopened boxes of TV figurines.
(I *am* the prick who laughs at priceless things.)

I *do* dress straight out of a Penney's catalog:
press my pants for fear you'll undress me.

I *did* land me a good girl. She loves to consider herself
a dream-catcher: I'm the feathery one.

I *can't* stop looking at the sky for promise.
I've spent life on the stars: betting at different angles.

AT THE MUSEUM OF NATURAL HISTORY

Bo Diddley's last words were not filled with gurgling
dark notes, throat melodic with the ache of Mississippi
currents, deeper than night's rocky banks, its weeping
magnolias. His thumbs simply sung towards heaven; he blinked.

I blink. I miss the name of one of two hands
that molded Second City into a Mecca of comedy.
A prayer was made, a candle vigil at Piper's Alley.
The next three minutes are an elementary teacher's,

shot in the head in her car, splattered in the shadow
of an alley. This is the closest we'll ever get to knowing
her story: invoking irony, invoking a deep ripping
in my stomach. The TV says her passion was stripping

guns from the suckling, angry hands of her unleashed
community. She tried to save children raised to hate pigs,
raised to hate the next block's colors: babies threatened
from chances to leave the street's umbilical cord.

Her death is another hinge in the cracked door, a peek
into the room which holds the city's ugly secrets. Her ending
will sit knotted into a tiny ball, buried in two days
in the paper's middle pages . . .

We can see the whites of their eyes like stars, if we want.
See them as unfathomable stars in a lampless cartoon scene . . .

At a traveling exhibit of Pompeii, we stroll through remnants
of earth, preserved in the neat term of *pyroclastic surge*.
The melt river of rock shards shot down the village.
The world quickly wet and hot.

The lava swallowed lives so fast that most towers
of human form fossilized. Each step through the exhibit
a new pose: hands reading the air, conducting painful
symphonies, the explosion their final movement.

Gawk at the shells of human shapes, some tucking
knees tight to chest; some with limbs
pumped into flight by adrenaline.
The idea of protection eroded in veins.

CATCHING BEAUTY

Matisse said that every country has its own
light, while the Les Halles butcher explained

each muscle has its own flavor
depending on nationality and feed.

A Greek painter can divide sunlight
into color, and colors into hues,

which is why he has a key to the church
to paint his humble *Michelangito*

when divinely moved. It's been 25 years
and he still works, and the orthodox

do not push for its end. You were given
your own key, able to distinguish the weather

by the scent of my wrist, the shallow cave
of my neck. I understand your temper

through your hands. If they are tired
you are tired. If your fingers volunteer

a walk through my hair, you're alive
and happy, even if you can't tell yourself

apart.

CHINESE LANTERN FESTIVAL

Painted folk tales are narrated at night, riddles
brushed with the delicacy of an archaeologist:

lanterns sing like magnolia petals, little monuments
planted on the riverbed of ledges, brighten city shadows.

My flame's blue finger extends, strokes the insides
with its nebula of light. Tracing the outer language,

I am careful not to tear the paper wall of our little house.
This is the year of the dog: I see your body

in the fluid body of a cyan dragon lurching
its decorated shoulders, set to pounce and clutch.

Where do you hide, beneath the current
of my hands? Digging a base need, we seek

artifacts our histories say exist. The full moon pulls us
from our sea beds: *kosmos* a myth: there's no order,

no harmony in the night's flickering embers. Just a trick
distance wraps our eyes around. Souls rise

from the stacks: the new year drawing out what's left
inside our rekindling, since you last tied

your hair back: a thick strand tickles the right
of your face, rests on your brow's gentle arch:

I brush softly, tuck it behind ear and kiss:
temple, forehead, temple.

THE ASTRONOMER AS BIRDER

Each sand grain is born
from 70 million, million,
million atoms.

Only *three* births
one water molecule:
the tiniest speck of life.

German scientists
forecast 500 billion galaxies
float in the universe.

And here, we have
the Wood Duck's call
sound like running

away, endless space echoes,
and the Lesser Scaup
swallowed

by the pond's black hole
in their dives, barely a ripple
left on the water's plane,

their hunt too deep
for the human eye.
Each little grit

caught in your beach teeth
could be a water planet
crashing out of orbit:

a cluster of galaxies
collapsing in the universe
of a gaping mouth.

THE LAST LIVING PRIMITIVES

The Yanomamo drink their dead. Our kindred
spirits, perhaps. The missing link somewhere

between Lucy and today's most vapid, Prufrockian
cyber-chap. We are like them, you and me,

our hearts fletched arrows, stabbing at the panic
of some dark Amazon – a wall of fauna, flora

to discover. Our wet lips decorate lips
and they paint their baskets with masticated

coal. But here they are, a primitive, encyclopedic
people, endorsing Toyota, riding backseat

in the Tundra cab, smiles wide as a cunning
(some may say *wacky*) rabbit.

This might be the proper time to announce
I see little difference in family portraits

of the Flintstones and the Jetsons,
who, of course, are cartoons in their own

nifty sorts of automobiles. When did the car
become society's climax? How did Geico

Insurance get America so right
with those "So simple a caveman can do it"

commercials? Here we are on the couch
being reduced to the lowest denominator:

I'll have you know I'm okay with anything
that breaks down the universe

into two dimensions, into an equation:
the us we know, and know

to some degree why we do what we do,
and the them we don't know, and don't know

because they're from "another place."
For instance, Yanonmami

drink the crushed bones
of dead relatives to keep them forever,

but they don't whisper their names.
They are mourning. They've not discovered

the wheel, and snort their hallucinogens
through giant, straw-like cane.

I almost forgot them until Toyota (through use,
probably, of some middle-class Brazilian

or Venezuelan stand-ins) brought them out
of the rainforest. I am thankful, for this

reminds me of us. Do take comfort
my little undertaker's daughter,

for when I touch you, they gossip.
If we lived among them, mouths would run

from remote village to river
and our deeds, fetched

in wooden buckets,
drunk.

PHYSIOLOGY

That we are made of oceans and rivulets
makes sense today. The sky has softly coughed
all afternoon:

If the body is not watered it will close down
its tiniest veins, blood thickened like preserves.

I believe my father kisses the dirt
the way pelts of rain kiss the wood railing
as the sky begins its swell:

The car is being washed for free!

For once, there's no bitterness
in baseball games at twelve never made up
after a downpour – the missed

two-dollar concession dog
dressed tightly in foil.

The rain lifts. It lifts.
I sense – like all working bodies –
the five ways earth accepts the rain:

indulges a mourning
dove as it plumps from thirst.

iii.

always inside me is the child who died,
always inside me is his will to die –

     – Robert Lowell,
        "Night Sweat"

I felt a Funeral, in my Brain,
And Mourners to and fro
Kept treading – treading – till it seemed
That Sense was breaking through –

     – Emily Dickinson,
        "I felt a Funeral,
         in my Brain"

SILENT DEFIANCE

It arose the year she burned down
the kitchen in a grease fire.
Decided to hide in the miles.
Took pills in a college town
while I read *Popular Mechanics*
and our greaser brother
slowly scrapped the Escort
as the limp summer air
nibbled at our dreams
of elsewhere.

Joe pocketed fifty for the alternator,
showed me how to remove
brake pads, until a bee shot
straight up my armpit.
An island rose on my skin
and I ran far as a touchy boy can –
across the Second St. Bridge –
where fishermen dotted the banks,
where bodies and poles dipped
in the Auglaize, reflected like ladles
in the river's backward sky.

Men splashed off their lines, dissolved
into the never-ending currents:
constellations in muddy space.

I thought of Rogelio's father
hiding in Texas, alive, a fleck
of salt on tortilla-burned land;
how this would make his boy churn
thick forest stumps for legs
on the football fields in Defiance:
each yard tearing up their likeness.

To Rogelio and me, girls only began
to taste – yes – like tender fire
peaches from the farmer's market:

it was our generation's turn at begging
to dance the obvious dance.

The summer like a pair of braces
quietly correcting futures, left us
with our mouths wired shut,
as we hoped to realign into something
worth admiring.

Soon, girls wrapped their arms
around the fresh muscle
of high school jocks – lucky
Rogelio – while I swung
through the last pages
of a Victorian novel, rooted
on the porch: obedient.

My brother slithered out the window each night:
hid his weed scales in a little wooden box;
his love notes and his love songs in a blue coffee tin.

I imagine my sister
picked at the plastic bracelet
with her name: her vitals ticked off
like time on a chronographic watch.

The hospital voices sewed a deep stitch
in her paper gown.

That same summer I first realized
rain's soft scent blooming on the wrists

of all the beautiful girls in town,
I also learned a shock
of wheat's a symbol of resurrection
in Ancient Egypt; that part of Osaka
can mean "return to soil";
that the bright red of blood
comes from oxygen – underneath
skin flows a suffocated color
akin to a sweet cherry, dark
down to its pit.

The porch became my best friend.

The yew bushes grew
into Japanese soldiers
and I started reading haiku. Drawn
to their common story, I scrawled.

> *Air a wet plum bit*
> *into with lovers. Bodies*
> *radiate sharp pine,*
>
> *two needles bristling*
> *against each other in wind.*
> *Morning's first red gasp,*
>
> *steals from his shadow,*
> *tip-toes on meditation*
> *rocks, back to the bed*
>
> *her husband commands.*
> *She weaves effortlessly, twig*
> *into nesting sheets,*
>
> *absence elusive*
> *and quick as the cherry blos-*
> *som. Dance on a branch.*

Our mother left work
to find her only daughter:
how our minds sneak off!

The warm navy sky
coiled its infinite arms
around each star

and hushed the engines
to a hum as we turned each
rustic, lifeless bend

fast down Route 15,
from Defiance to Findlay –
small towns throbbing pulses –

that familiar glow
of June bugs drowning in pools:
wet nights cue the lungs.

1988: ACCIDENTAL

The canal locks were weak knees.
His birthday a day away, he waxed
poetic – took in his only son – a crow
shot itself out of the light, cawed all the way
down to the water. Did he really breathe
in fatherhood? Was he fishing, or just fish
food? The cops and everyone else play hangman
with modest facts. *Unsolved Mysteries* calls once
more than his mother ever did while he lived.
Absent a DeLorean, the detective favors bad luck
and the fluvial process – a sharp rift
in the lock – body eroding over the years
as the river washes to the bay. It didn't help
his inhaler was his most trusted friend.
My mother locked in a timeless rift
with his mother. Jealousy over a man
who owns them both. And we pay
and we pay with all the blame: death
accrues on our souls, thickens like algae.

TO FAILURE:

     I never wanted to be an astronaut, suffocated
by thought: all that tethers a man to ship is ingenuity
and wiring.
     Never a doctor, for all the skin
I've split open, each scar's lip chatter
a permanent marker of foolishness:
     How I kicked my way out of brotherhood
fights; lifted more than I should to impress
all those beautiful girls who valued me more
as a good listener, because I could repeat back
like a tape recorder, the important phrases.
     How I wanted to be Indiana Jones, his whole cowboy-
professor balancing act – to ruggedly flex my intellect –
tripping over *Australopithecus* and *patriarchal society*
in bar conversations, house warming parties
and baby showers.
     You're unavoidable, I hear an old lady
on the train whisper: like fire once it realizes
it can breathe, you prey on the world, leave us all
self-described martyrs in our own ashes.
     By now, I should be loudly objecting
to the needling pleas of aunts who still believe
I want to go to law school. Who beg me to forget
about writing books and be happy simply
correcting the mixing of past and present tense;
suggesting changes in the vagaries of somethings
and someones in the midnight scripts of adrenaline-
rushed youth, their worlds half constructed
in night's silent race with dawn.
     Raised fatherless and slight, uncles
want me to roughen my *pretty* hands, deaden
a few layers at work in the same daily dark
they live – await factory downsizes in drinking
clubs named after better animals than man,

where it's all gamble on football and gobble
the remnants from cracked peanut shells
piling in glass cigarette trays.

MOST WANTED

Battle of the Bay, October 17, 1989

Show me where to put my hands
perfectly on the bat the girl the drill

Show me how to grip a beer
unconsciously unpretentiously

and feel like I belong in the clan
taking jabs at one another

massaging each others' shoulders
with enough torque to power stockcars

I would die to have fingers
that open fault lines, tear down

an entire city, stop a World Series
long enough we always forget

who has won and who has lost

TO THE HOUSEPAINTER:

A winter-fat robin pecks at snow
over the empty granite marker –
your name chiseled into little canals –

your body broken down by fire
into ashes, jarred
at Riverview Gardens – ironic,

considering you were crippled
by open air; by lungs
that couldn't handle pollen

or the flame of human voices –

couldn't handle your love
smoking her pack-a-day of Salems.

The problem isn't that you died
so early in your life. It's that you died
so early in mine.

I offer the name of my first-born
to know you better, longer: What sacrifice

buried in your chest? Anxiety
tucked up your flannel sleeves?

Did you love wet licks of fall
on your tongue? The cornmeal sun.

Do I say now – the pink and orange blurs
to a sweet violet night – that god's
a Van Gogh fan –

for light dances at a rhythmic speed
our eyes only blur what's left?

My brother taught me how to hook
a worm – its raspberry and butter insides –
my sister, how a doll can speak.

HIS BODY A WEATHERED MAP

Obsession the wrong word:
more like uranium, long half-life,
poisonous, inevitable. *A ghost*

regenerates in brain cells,
you said, declaring
you'd stop breathing in

lines off an old TV,
absorbing Mickey Mouse's smile
from sheets.

Tragedy, a hallucination
always has a downfall.
Want is a god-damned chainsaw,

the pain a Redwood.
I remember the first step, listening
to those poor bastards

lack control, sentenced
to AA. But I admire my son
and grasp it's addiction

carving a father
out of police reports, news
clippings. You declare yours

a swimming sperm donor
in a sea of women. Billy's: a 2x4
and the hammer

and the nails. Sarah
watched from on top
the basement's creaky stairs

as hers daintily dipped toothpicks
in glue, scanned his little town
for where to put the skating rink.

She gets lost in the boy in red
scarf, where all she ever wanted –
so simple – was to steal

his snow-bright face
as the train whistled and chugged
its way around a happy world.

1988: MURDER, AGAIN

She sends church
pamphlets with her
poetry in it. Grandma
a strange tongue
metaphors swim off
with Aesop's horses
or where rabbits pillage
carrots from a baby
garden. Her son scattered
from fire to air to earth to water.
She sends a camel's back
of more obvious verse
that preaches borders
between our lives:
Heaven and Earth;
Love versus Hate.
I write in my journal:
The esophagus can swell
to an unrecognizable
muscle. Lungs absent
surfactant collapse
like whoopee cushions.
A wind whispers around
town: she pushed him
over the edge, literally,
after she split him
from my mother.
My window wheezes
in the fabled dark: she sold
his house and pickup, contract-
ions of guilt and acceptance,
faithless in the most faithful.
There was no discovery
of his body, yet: the Great Wall
still to fall between two indefinite

Berlins. When the news
anchor breached the dam:
his name swelled
my ears and throat, collapsed
the foundation worn
on my shoulders: the mule
that's broken, grain sacks
thieved.

CHURCHES

Kutna Horá, Czech Republic

We tour the bone church, first, as the sun breaks
out of its earthly grave. The sanctuary named
after a medievalist who stripped plague victims
to their indecent whites and decorated sacred
with his artistic fetish. A half-blind Cistercian
monk used the newborn church as his palette;
the walls clean as light, he rummaged the cemetery
for supplies, antique bones washed of flesh:
a yard fertile long before the church, the ground
a pilgrimage for death, we are told: an abbot sprinkled
earth from Golgotha unto his land, and soon
the plots grew into religious fashion. The craze
of late fourteenth century. I walk the moss-rugged
burial path as Matt, a near seven-foot man, dangles
his spidery legs over the wall, having taken a piss
on its other side, his back to a playground slide.
I repeat how the church was erected after the rolling
death counts, in the heart of headstones: what was quarried
for the foundation was mixed like a bucket of chicken
with fresh refugee bones; sculpted into pinnacles, monstrances.
For the first time, I light a candle in church, donate
money, stare up at the chandelier, deadened, and count
all two hundred and six bones in the human body.

Our next place of worship, in the hazy afternoon,
is gated. Its original fence circles the hill, holds
better than the wall-scaling snails, their shells
hollowed by light hitting the open land. Only a fist
of people fit inside to see the never-used tomb
upfront in a barren room. Outside
two sweat bees rest stiffly on their backs in yellow
weed-flowers, their bodies like emptied jars.
Three men kick a soccer ball back and forth
over a tennis net on the clay court downhill. Somehow
there's more life in their feet, the sun hanging
like a lantern over a distant village, while our party
complains we're tired of the countryside's heat.

NECROPOLIS

Underneath Paris and Rome stew the gristly parts
of two ancient cities. In *Futurama*, the Big Apple
becomes a septic tank to an alien city above it.
JFK sent us to space to look for space. It seems
civilization's constant is real estate. What remains
of uninhabited land is where Darwin knows
we could not survive making home. Unless, of course,
we make the land adapt to us, bring in steamrollers
and such, drive out the penguins and the Inuit,
the Bedouin and the Amazonians. Or go back to caves
near Jerusalem, where eight new species were found
alive, millions of years in their own world. The chalky
armor of white scorpion-like creatures half-buried
on a sand battlefield, this world, unearthed. Nowhere
to put the dead to rest unless we burn them.

THE MOON CLINGS TO THE MORNING

We spend nights holding on to the buckle of Orion's belt
and mornings looking down at the fiery glitter

of the river's midnight-blue road; its spread up to those giants
for buildings – tearing nothing, barely
touching the Chicago skyline

like a child of ten, waist high
but grabbing at the power in his father's
rough shape, his face.

We find ourselves wrapped
around our own earths, like glass and light
clinging for decades to steel girders

cemented at depth – measured.
What's an architect with no blueprints?

No old man to ramp up against
on shivering black nights;

no second law
of motion to react to.

There is silence at dawn when the sky aches
with its pulsing bruise, open as a desert.

Will we ever find that place – oasis
still solid when the clouds shift –

no tricks to keep us lonely as the stars,
the false lines drawn in constellations?

TO JAMES WRIGHT:

I hold her for everything, measure
kisses on her forehead. Crawling
with illusions: her head slammed
against the floor as her parents play
Roman jury, verdict sealed:
    I confess this nightmare
to her womb, drenched in the swell
of April thunder.
    At my age, the body's rolling voltage
threw father into the clouds, rewired
by drugs, genetics,
    and nobody can forecast
where lightning strikes. The aftermath:
    Mother dissipating into sky
like a fly ball, flayed in the polarity –
children left to men with shotgun
mouths, derelict tongues, scattered
to corners of rooms.
    Tornadoes inhaled us,
spit us out like chew, clumps
of hair clumps of grass – nothing
untouched in their paths.
    Decades, I've battled these cannons
looser than the wind, rebuilding
a tattered landscape, afraid
the violence that anchors memories
won't stay asleep in my dreams.
    I want to contain the animal, not even
let it be a breeze on the face of my loves.
    When I read your scripture
wet with drink, with the wretched
redeemed – still, words never quite repair
what they repair.
    How do you think boys last
the climate – rebirth from droughts

of whiskey, manic falls
back into bed,
      banished to the heavenly
nightmares of life?

TO OCD:

My fear: pliancy
    of flesh, structural
boundaries. Daily reminders

in failed love-making
from a cramp or the swayed backs
of seniors

      being anchored to earth:

where the body admits
we are nothing like Atlas, holding up the sky,

even if we name a neck bone after him.

A seizure rolling through
the dog: an earthquake shaking family
      predictably out of control.
The vet says she doesn't feel
a thing, but we coddle her
      in our knowledge: meager
                arms. Our bodies fantasies
the surface sloshed away
over the years: cells of what we were: somehow invisible, fluid
memory, retained.

To be
      the dog: forget
there has to be a left and right sock, spines
of books color-coded, albums alphabetized
by recording studio:
              for harmony. To forgo belief

the thirty-two chew cycle will save me.

Forced to repeat the same sequence before shutting off
                        the shower, to unchain oneself from drowning

in a set of numbers that masters each day.

THE GOLDEN ONE

There are things I can't open
my mouth to. You say: the frozen Maumee
shines like El Dorado. I tease: the Ohio
city, or Colombia's myth? This state of obvious
seasons, that fakes worship of the sun
with towns named Texas, Florida, Nevada.
I deflect: there are whole worlds under the ice.
I think: my father was tossed around like clothes
in a washer; the river's color of childhood
knee stains. Hunters found his carcass. You say:
these snake turns make me nauseous – did you see
that semi bull around the bend? I think: I must protect
you, the dog, the unborn baby I want to know
his father. I tell you what I'm not thinking: as kids
we gave each other ruthless nicknames – Bucky
Sprout, Niagara Nose and Split Tooth Ugly; we called
him Rob the Slob because he wiped paint-splatter
of a day's work all over an embroidered handkerchief.
I keep to myself: my father was a Zipa, dusted with earth
and gold to be received as king of a lost world.

SON:

You counted three languages
on my hand to learn the world
is full of rhythms:

one, two, three / une,
deux trois / uno,
dos, tres.

Your tongue is a wand.
Brotherhood shimmers
in shapes of sound.

Your mother surrendered
her body for you: never argue
sacrifice isn't love's

primary definition. At first,
you cut each day
into two-hour segments,

like the bread factory
in summers where the foreman
sliced shifts into portions

we could swallow the heat.
Someday a lover will give you up
for another. Someday a lover

will come back from the rain.
You will ask for advice; I will fail
making sense of the senseless.

Our bodies lack capacity to reason
pain. I cannot always protect you
from Nigerian princes, long lost dead

European heiresses. Duck and weave
like my dad showed me, five, knuckles
wrapped. The world is a fist:

a swollen nose stings
through the eyes; learn to breathe
it all in, counter and defend.

[I SOLEMNLY] SWEAR

You will not see a woman transform into eagle
and shred the cheek neck forearms of a poacher.

You will not think a shriek freedom – we are free
as talons that rip skin off the body like air.

You will be hidden from merry-go-round men
who play out their homes with drinks.

With paycheck threats. With mop handles
doubling as 'toys.'

You will not know frozen tile like a bear trap
where all you hear are the familiar canals

pulsing your own ears. You will never be tossed
like dirty laundry. Your mother will never be

a kicked-at rat, chased to the humming blue walls
pale as winter that squint eyes in fluorescence.

The trick called shelter: you will not hear those babies
whimper from fattened mouths,

hummingbirds in hurricanes no Doppler can predict.
The brain must be set like a bone:

even the special healing powers of youth. For this,
there is one unflinching law in our house:

We will not use tongues fists bats guns
to accelerate the body's uselessness to another.

ENTROPY

My son will one day ask,
Where is your father?

I will be a lost puppy in his cartoons
       I will draw an equation in sidewalk chalk

so simple I will beg a storm
to wash it away

We are all that guy who simply cannot say
what he means to say
or knows he should say

A quarter century since he last breathed in
this world,
          perhaps he lives

in the eternity I have no interest in

Each year his myth more obese

          like a nebula cloud,
             thick layers of dust clustering
         in the false quiet of space

Perhaps I'll call him a planet
       That is exactly how I see him

Perhaps I will call him the entropy
       to the thermodynamics of my soul,

the unavailable energy   never again matter

Isn't that what the dead do to the living

Death never flushes
from the system
                    like car oil, drugs, virus
Valves scar, our piping rusts,
                    used or not

So like the tides, the moon to the earth,
his anniversary catalyzes

a season of beautiful weather patterns,
            a mist that glistens the pied-beauty of a fall

To absorb in silence a black hole, I will tell my boy
what any sentimental fool should,
only half joking:

            that mine is hiding under the hull
                    of my chest, in the orbital
                    of my eye

because he will not understand this,
            and neither will I, and nobody,

not even the young,
            will keep asking

FATHER BELONGS TO THE RIVER

And not to the gun-slinging shadow sitting
shotgun in a brown banana-boat at the drive-thru
bank.
    Or the teller whose unsure voice
was the last person known to see him breathing.
Or the rust-mottled fishing tackle also warping
on his back porch. Or the inhaler used to pry
his esophagus open, skillful as a cat
burglar letting in the wind.
    Or his mother, whose bob
was always a little suspicious.
    Or his father who died when I was weeks
into this world. Or my mother who loved him
too late, and is stuck justifying her lost
love to her adult son.
    And every visit there is less and less
mentioning of how he once stole back
everything he'd bought her, his blood
shot with a swig of jealousy at some man
my mom never dated, or fucked.
    It occurs to me, the infamous couch
my sister always speaks of, taken as well,
serves as backdrop in the sepia
of a year old me and a fractured him
on all fours in a happy moment.
    But he doesn't belong to me, captured
bucking at life; the picture nothing
but a picture of a time I am too young.
I did not know him as my father, only
understood his love through touches
which kept my little body from trouble.
    And he is not owned by my aunt
who paid for the lawyer who settled his life
into a number, handed to my mother
in monthly installments.

And he is not owned by the factories
for which he paid his time in hot darkness.
    And he is not owned by the story
of his disappearance, or the stories
of his death.
    And the father I want remains
a collage, badly constructed, sticky, fluid
as the Maumee, which took him and kept him
until, inside, I knew he was dead.
    And his body remains the earth's,
though his bones pour out memories.
    And when he is ash
he is ash and he is licked by every tongue
of wind this town has ever seen.

NOTES

The title "When I Was A Boy The Sun Was A Horse" comes from a line in James Reiss' "¿Habla Usted Español?" from his first collection, *The Breathers*.

The italicized lines in "The Boundaries Of Science" are from a Bill Joy article, "Why the Future Doesn't Need Us."

www.ingramcontent.com/pod-product-compliance
Lightning Source LLC
Chambersburg PA
CBHW031145090426
42738CB00008B/1227